The Mindset Accountability Journal

40 DAYS TO A NEW YOU

ALLIE HUDSON

LUCIDBOOKS

The Mindset Accountability Journal
40 Days to a New You

Copyright © 2018 by Allie Hudson
Published by Lucid Books in Houston, TX
www.LucidBooksPublishing.com

All rights reserved. No part of this publication may be reproduced, stored in a retrieval system, or transmitted in any form by any means, electronic, mechanical, photocopy, recording, or otherwise, without the prior permission of the publisher, except as provided for by USA copyright law.

ISBN-10: 1-63296-302-7
ISBN-13: 978-1-63296-302-4
eISBN-10: 1-6296-262-4
eISBN-13: 978-1-63296-262-1

Special Sales: Most Lucid Books titles are available in special quantity discounts. Custom imprinting or excerpting can also be done to fit special needs. Contact Lucid Books at Info@LucidBooksPublishing.com.

I would like to dedicate this book to my parents, Albert and Anna Koch, who have always told me I could do anything I put my mind to. I would also like to thank Mike Olencki for his support and encouragement to be the best person I can be. You are my best friend and my rock.

Thank you to Tara Sotirin for taking my scribbles and making them into a great design. Thank you to my encouragers Roxy Jordet and Amy Polak who encouraged me to pursue this dream.

Introduction

Welcome! This is the first step in **The Mindset Accountability Journal,** a 40-day journey to becoming your truest self by achieving a Mindset of Gratitude.

I have always been fascinated by the butterfly and how, through its metamorphosis, it changes from an ugly worm into a beautiful insect. It flies free and brings so much beauty to our lives. This journal is the beginning of your metamorphosis. It may not seem like this small change, spending 30 minutes a day working on your inner self, can change your life so much, **BUT IT WILL.**

If you talk to or read about any successful person, you will discover a connection—they will discuss and focus on gratitude. They may discuss it in different ways, but many of them attribute a major part of their success to their focus on gratitude. Personally, I am inspired by Chrissy Metz of *This Is Us* fame and her journey involving gratitude. She spends every morning focusing on five things that she is grateful for in her life, even if it is just thanking God for her eyesight.[1] It seems like a small change, but focusing on gratitude makes

---
1. Chrissy Metz, *This Is Me* (New York: Harper Collins, 2018), 62–63.

a major difference in how you experience your life. Many other actors talk about gratitude in their lives and careers as well. Actor Densel Washington contributes his major success in life to his focus on gratitude.[2]

T. Harv Eker talks about how to address problems in your life in his book *Secrets of the Millionaire Mind*. He reminds us that you can't do anything about the fruit on the tree; instead, you have to change the root of your issue.[3] That is exactly what I found on my own journey. When I started my journey toward a Mindset of Gratitude, the small things I was grateful for began to change many of the big issues in my life. Through my journey and my new mindset, I began to appreciate my husband again. I began to appreciate the opportunity to develop my skills. I began to overcome my fears and start living my life.

> **You must make a commitment to spend time every day for the next 40 days focusing on and developing your inner person.**

---

2. Denzel Washington, "Put God First," *YouTube*, https://www.youtube.com/watch?v=BxY_eJLBflk.
3. T. Harv Eker, *Secrets of the Millionaire Mind* (New York: Harper Business, 2005), 12–13.

This is how I suggest that you use this journal:

• Spend 5 to 10 minutes every day focusing on five things that make you feel grateful.

• Read or listen to 15 minutes of self-development; write a response in the mindset reading section.

• Paul Solomon, professed psychic and seer, advises to pick one concept that you learn from your reading or audio. Then say to yourself, "I can. I will. I do. I am." You realize you need to be more positive in your daily outlook in life. So say to yourself, "I **can** be positive with each thing I do daily," "I **will** be positive no matter what happens today," "I **do** live my life positively on a daily basis," "I **am** a positive person who sees the best in everyone I meet and every circumstance that comes my way."[4]

Doing these things will slowly begin to change your mindset from where you are right now to where you want to be and help you visualize who you are going to become.

I challenge you to follow this path daily with whatever concept you have learned for the day.

I know that there will be days when you don't get this done first thing in the morning, which is the best time to continue the journey. If you miss a couple

---

4. Paul Solomon, "Self-Talk," July 20, 2015, https://www.youtube.com/watch?v=z4fxj97GNKk&app=desktop.

days, pick back up where you would have been, and then go back and get the other days when you are able. The most important part is to push yourself forward. Making this a daily a habit is the most important change to make to your life. Make it a priority. If it is the only thing you get done, then don't worry. You can even use this in conjunction with your daily devotion and prayers. But learning to move from daily living to grateful living will make a big change in your life. It will help you make the choices to move forward.

So get going!

Make this your priority for the next 40 days. I look forward to hearing from you about how your outlook on life has changed.

Tips for Journaling

Write EVERY DAY, even if it is just a small response or a quick idea. Go back and refine ideas that you want to expand on later.

Write in the morning before your mind is filled with the daily distractions.

Write slowly at a speed that gives you time to think as you write.

Choose a writing utensil that is easy to write with and that you like to use.

Look back and read some of your previous entries and continue or refine some of your writings.

Use the things you learn about yourself from your journal to change your daily life.

The Mindset
Accountability Journal

40 DAYS TO A NEW YOU

Date:

Gratitude Log

1. _____

_____

2. _____

_____

3. _____

_____

4. _____

_____

5. _____

_____

Day One

If you really want to change your mindset, you have to start somewhere. **Today is the day.** One step at a time. Commit yourself to the next 40 days.

Day: /40

Mindset Reading — Log

Read at least 30 minutes.
Write your one takeaway from that reading.

_____
_____
_____
_____
_____
_____
_____

Inspire

If your actions inspire others to dream more, learn more, do more and become more, you are a leader.
—John Quincy Adams

Action for Mindset Change

Date:

Gratitude Log

1. _____

_____

2. _____

_____

3. _____

_____

4. _____

_____

5. _____

_____

Day Two

It's an accomplishment that you came back.
Give yourself a win!

Day: /40

Mindset Reading — Log

Read at least 30 minutes.
Write your one takeaway from that reading.

_____

_____

_____

_____

_____

_____

_____

Inspire

Enjoy the little things, for one day you may look back and realize they were the big things.
—Robert Brault

Action for Mindset Change

Date:

Gratitude Log

1. _____

_____

2. _____

_____

3. _____

_____

4. _____

_____

5. _____

_____

Day Three

Never fail to recognize the
Beginning of something **Great**.

Day: /40

Mindset Reading | Log

Read at least 30 minutes.
Write your one takeaway from that reading.

_____
_____
_____
_____
_____
_____
_____

Inspire

Knowing is not enough; we must apply.
Willing is not enough; we must do.
—Johann Wolfgang von Goethe

Action for Mindset Change

Date:

Gratitude Log

1. _____

_____

2. _____

_____

3. _____

_____

4. _____

_____

5. _____

_____

Day Four

You may not feel it, but it **is** making a difference.

Day: /40

Mindset Reading | Log

Read at least 30 minutes.
Write your one takeaway from that reading.

_____

_____

_____

_____

_____

_____

Inspire

> Nothing can stop the man with the right mental attitude from achieving his goal; nothing on earth can help the man with the wrong mental attitude.
> —Thomas Jefferson

Action for Mindset Change

Date:

Gratitude Log

1. _____
_____

2. _____
_____

3. _____
_____

4. _____
_____

5. _____
_____

Day Five

Keep going!
You are doing great.

Day: /40

Mindset Reading | Log

Read at least 30 minutes.
Write your one takeaway from that reading.

_____

_____

_____

_____

_____

_____

Inspire

> For success, attitude is equally as important as ability.
> —Walter Scott

Action for Mindset Change

Date:

Gratitude Log

1. _____

2. _____

3. _____

4. _____

5. _____

Day Six

It's the little practices that make the most difference.

Day: /40

Mindset Reading — Log

Read at least 30 minutes.
Write your one takeaway from that reading.

_____

_____

_____

_____

_____

_____

Inspire

Wise men speak because they have something to say; Fools because they have to say something.
—Plato

Action for Mindset Change

Date:

Gratitude Log

1. _____

_____

2. _____

_____

3. _____

_____

4. _____

_____

5. _____

_____

Day Seven

One Week! Congratulations!
Be proud of yourself.

Day: /40

Mindset Reading — Log

Read at least 30 minutes.
Write your one takeaway from that reading.

_____

_____

_____

_____

_____

_____

Inspire

> Beware of missing chances; otherwise it may be altogether too late some day.
> **–Franz Liszt**

Action for Mindset Change

Date:

Gratitude Log

1. _____

_____

2. _____

_____

3. _____

_____

4. _____

_____

5. _____

_____

Day Eight

Starting to feel different now?

Day: /40

Mindset Reading — Log

Read at least 30 minutes.
Write your one takeaway from that reading.

_____

_____

_____

_____

_____

_____

Inspire

The greatest test of courage on earth is to bear defeat without losing heart.
—Robert Green Ingersoll

Action for Mindset Change

Date:

Gratitude Log

1. _____
   _____

2. _____
   _____

3. _____
   _____

4. _____
   _____

5. _____
   _____

Day Nine

Can you write each journal entry without having to struggle?

Day: /40

Mindset Reading — Log

Read at least 30 minutes.
Write your one takeaway from that reading.

_____

_____

_____

_____

_____

_____

Inspire

A great man does not seek applause or place; he seeks for truth; he seeks the road to happiness, and what he ascertains, he gives to others.

—Robert Green Ingersoll

Action for Mindset Change

Date:

Gratitude Log

1. _____

2. _____

3. _____

4. _____

5. _____

Day Ten

It was at this point that I really noticed a change.

| Day: | /40 |

◯ Mindset Reading — Log

Read at least 30 minutes.
Write your one takeaway from that reading.

_____

_____

_____

_____

_____

_____

Inspire

> Happiness is the only good.
> The time to be happy is now. The place to be happy is here. The way to be happy is to make others so.
> **—Robert Green Ingersoll**

◯ Action for Mindset Change

✓ *10* DAYS

Great Job!

You have committed to changing your mindset and, by doing that, committed to changing your life for the better.

Date:

Gratitude Log

1. _____

_____

2. _____

_____

3. _____

_____

4. _____

_____

5. _____

_____

Day Eleven

The habit is starting to develop.
Keep going!

Day: ___ /40

● Mindset Reading — Log

Read at least 30 minutes.
Write your one takeaway from that reading.

_____

_____

_____

_____

_____

_____

Inspire

Experience is the teacher of all things.
—Julius Caesar

● Action for Mindset Change

Date:

Gratitude Log

1. _____
   _____

2. _____
   _____

3. _____
   _____

4. _____
   _____

5. _____
   _____

Day Twelve

Missed a day?
Don't worry. Just catch up later.

Day: /40

Mindset Reading | Log

Read at least 30 minutes.
Write your one takeaway from that reading.

_____

_____

_____

_____

_____

_____

_____

Inspire

Life is the continuous adjustment of internal relations to external relations.
—Herbert Spencer

Action for Mindset Change

Date:

Gratitude Log

1. _____
_____

2. _____
_____

3. _____
_____

4. _____
_____

5. _____
_____

Day Thirteen

I love that you are sticking with it!

Day: /40

Mindset Reading | Log

Read at least 30 minutes.
Write your one takeaway from that reading.

_____

_____

_____

_____

_____

_____

Inspire

> The great aim of education is not knowledge but action.
> **—Herbert Spencer**

Action for Mindset Change

Date:

Gratitude Log

1. _____

_____

2. _____

_____

3. _____

_____

4. _____

_____

5. _____

_____

Day Fourteen

Two Weeks!
Can you believe it?
You are committed to making this work.

Day: ___ /40

Mindset Reading Log

Read at least 30 minutes.
Write your one takeaway from that reading.

_____
_____
_____
_____
_____
_____

Inspire

It is the mark of an educated mind to be able to entertain a thought without accepting it.
—Aristotle

Action for Mindset Change

Date:

Gratitude Log

1. _____
   _____
2. _____
   _____
3. _____
   _____
4. _____
   _____
5. _____
   _____

Day Fifteen

Commit to win.

Day: /40

● Mindset Reading — Log

Read at least 30 minutes.
Write your one takeaway from that reading.

_____

_____

_____

_____

_____

_____

Inspire

> A person often meets his destiny on the road he took to avoid it.
> **—Jean de La Fontaine**

● Action for Mindset Change

Date:

Gratitude Log

1. _____

_____

2. _____

_____

3. _____

_____

4. _____

_____

5. _____

_____

Day Sixteen

Almost halfway there!

Day: /40

Mindset Reading — Log

Read at least 30 minutes.
Write your one takeaway from that reading.

_____

_____

_____

_____

_____

_____

Inspire

> True happiness is to enjoy the present,
> without anxious dependence upon the future.
> **—Lucius Annaeus Seneca**

Action for Mindset Change

Date:

Gratitude Log

1. _____

_____

2. _____

_____

3. _____

_____

4. _____

_____

5. _____

_____

Day Seventeen

I knew you could do it.

Day: /40

Mindset Reading — Log

Read at least 30 minutes.
Write your one takeaway from that reading.

_____

_____

_____

_____

_____

_____

Inspire

> Surplus wealth is a sacred trust
> which its possessor is bound to administer in his
> lifetime for the good of the community.
> **—Andrew Carnegie**

Action for Mindset Change

Date:

Gratitude | Log

1. _____

2. _____

3. _____

4. _____

5. _____

Day Eighteen

This is going to be life-changing.

Day: /40

○ Mindset Reading · Log

Read at least 30 minutes.
Write your one takeaway from that reading.

_____
_____
_____
_____
_____
_____

Inspire

As I grow older, I pay less attention to what men say.
I just watch what they do.
—Andrew Carnegie

○ Action for Mindset Change

Date:

Gratitude Log

1. _____
   _____

2. _____
   _____

3. _____
   _____

4. _____
   _____

5. _____
   _____

Day Nineteen

You're still doing it, and that's amazing.

Day: /40

Mindset Reading — Log

Read at least 30 minutes.
Write your one takeaway from that reading.

_____

_____

_____

_____

_____

_____

Inspire

Do not take life too seriously.
You will never get out of it alive.
—Elbert Hubbard

Action for Mindset Change

Date:

Gratitude Log

1. _____

_____

2. _____

_____

3. _____

_____

4. _____

_____

5. _____

_____

Day Twenty

Halfway point! Now you know.

Day: /40

Mindset Reading — Log

Read at least 30 minutes.
Write your one takeaway from that reading.

_____

_____

_____

_____

_____

_____

Inspire

Happiness is the meaning and the purpose of life, the whole aim and end of human existence.
—Aristotle

Action for Mindset Change

Halfway There!

You should feel the changes in your life. Look back at where you started and think about where you would like to be in the next 20 days. Make the changes now!

Date:

Gratitude Log

1. _____

   _____

2. _____

   _____

3. _____

   _____

4. _____

   _____

5. _____

   _____

Day Twenty-One

Officially made the habit. Now it's time to ingrain it.

Day: /40

Mindset Reading — Log

Read at least 30 minutes.
Write your one takeaway from that reading.

_____

_____

_____

_____

_____

_____

Inspire

> Reflect upon your present blessings,
> of which every man has plenty; not on your past
> misfortunes, of which all men have some.
> **—Charles Dickens**

Action for Mindset Change

Date:

Gratitude Log

1. _____

_____

2. _____

_____

3. _____

_____

4. _____

_____

5. _____

_____

Day Twenty-Two

Being thankful is becoming easier.

Day: /40

Mindset Reading — Log

Read at least 30 minutes.
Write your one takeaway from that reading.

_____

_____

_____

_____

_____

_____

_____

Inspire

Acknowledging the good that you already have in your life is the foundation for all abundance.
—Eckhart Tolle

Action for Mindset Change

Date:

Gratitude Log

1. _____

   _____

2. _____

   _____

3. _____

   _____

4. _____

   _____

5. _____

   _____

Day Twenty-Three

Think of how you can encourage another person every day.

Day: /40

Mindset Reading — Log

Read at least 30 minutes.
Write your one takeaway from that reading.

_____
_____
_____
_____
_____
_____

Inspire

Gratitude...turns what we have into enough, and more. It turns denial into acceptance, chaos into order, confusion to clarity. Gratitude makes sense of our past, brings peace for today, and creates a vision for tomorrow.

—Melody Beattie

Action for Mindset Change

Date:

Gratitude Log

1. _____

_____

2. _____

_____

3. _____

_____

4. _____

_____

5. _____

_____

Day Twenty-Four

Send a text to someone you love. Tell them something you are grateful for about them.

Day: /40

○ Mindset Reading — Log

Read at least 30 minutes.
Write your one takeaway from that reading.

_____

_____

_____

_____

_____

_____

Inspire

Gratitude is a currency that we can mint for ourselves,
and spend without fear of bankruptcy.
—Fred De Witt Van Amburgh

○ Action for Mindset Change

Date:

Gratitude Log

1. _____

_____

2. _____

_____

3. _____

_____

4. _____

_____

5. _____

_____

Day Twenty-Five

Life is looking more positive these days.

Day: /40

⬤ Mindset Reading | Log

Read at least 30 minutes.
Write your one takeaway from that reading.

_____
_____
_____
_____
_____
_____

Inspire

At times, our own light goes out and is rekindled by a spark from another person. Each of us has cause to think with deep gratitude of those who have lighted the flame within us.

—Albert Schweitzer

⬤ Action for Mindset Change

Date:

Gratitude Log

1. _____

_____

2. _____

_____

3. _____

_____

4. _____

_____

5. _____

_____

Day Twenty-Six

Write a letter or note to someone you admire and let them know why.

Day: /40

Mindset Reading — Log

Read at least 30 minutes.
Write your one takeaway from that reading.

_____

_____

_____

_____

_____

_____

Inspire

Silent gratitude isn't very much to anyone.
—Gertrude Stein

Action for Mindset Change

Date:

Gratitude Log

1. _____
   _____

2. _____
   _____

3. _____
   _____

4. _____
   _____

5. _____
   _____

Day Twenty-Seven

Gratefulness is starting to show.

Day: /40

Mindset Reading | Log

Read at least 30 minutes.
Write your one takeaway from that reading.

_____

_____

_____

_____

_____

_____

_____

> **Inspire**
>
> Things turn out best for the people who make the best of the way things turn out.
> **–John Wooden**

Action for Mindset Change

Date:

Gratitude Log

1. _____

_____

2. _____

_____

3. _____

_____

4. _____

_____

5. _____

_____

Day Twenty-Eight

Have you told yourself how proud you are of yourself today? Do it now!

Day: ___ /40

Mindset Reading — Log

Read at least 30 minutes.
Write your one takeaway from that reading.

_____
_____
_____
_____
_____
_____
_____

Inspire

> Gratitude is the fairest blossom which springs from the soul.
> **—Henry Ward Beecher**

Action for Mindset Change

Date:

Gratitude Log

1. _____
_____

2. _____
_____

3. _____
_____

4. _____
_____

5. _____
_____

Day Twenty-Nine

May have missed a couple of days, but you made them up.

| Day: | /40 |

Mindset Reading — Log

Read at least 30 minutes.
Write your one takeaway from that reading.

_____

_____

_____

_____

_____

_____

Inspire

Gratitude is the memory of the heart.
—Jean-Baptiste Massieu

Action for Mindset Change

Date:

Gratitude Log

1. _____

_____

2. _____

_____

3. _____

_____

4. _____

_____

5. _____

_____

Day Thirty

Gratefulness flows a little more each day.

Day: /40

Mindset Reading Log

Read at least 30 minutes.
Write your one takeaway from that reading.

_____

_____

_____

_____

_____

_____

Inspire

> Gratitude is a quality similar to electricity;
> it must be produced and discharged and used up in order
> to exist at all.
>
> **—William Faulkner**

Action for Mindset Change

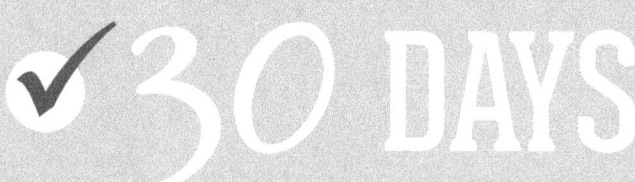

Amazing!

That's how you should feel today.
Thirty days of grateful living accomplished.
Ten days to go in this journal.

Date:

Gratitude Log

1. _____
_____

2. _____
_____

3. _____
_____

4. _____
_____

5. _____
_____

Day Thirty-One

It is amazing how your heart is singing this morning.

Day: /40

Mindset Reading — Log

Read at least 30 minutes.
Write your one takeaway from that reading.

_____

_____

_____

_____

_____

_____

Inspire

> There are always flowers for those who want to see them.
> **—Henri Matisse**

Action for Mindset Change

Date:

Gratitude Log

1. _____

_____

2. _____

_____

3. _____

_____

4. _____

_____

5. _____

_____

Day Thirty-Two

Love that you made it this far.
Most people won't!

Day: /40

Mindset Reading — Log

Read at least 30 minutes.
Write your one takeaway from that reading.

_____

_____

_____

_____

_____

_____

Inspire

Appreciation is a wonderful thing. It makes what is excellent in others belong to us as well.
—Voltaire

Action for Mindset Change

Date:

Gratitude Log

1. _____

_____

2. _____

_____

3. _____

_____

4. _____

_____

5. _____

_____

Day Thirty-Three

Only one week left in the journal, but don't forget, this is a lifestyle change.

Day: ___ /40

⬤ Mindset Reading │ Log

Read at least 30 minutes.
Write your one takeaway from that reading.

_____

_____

_____

_____

_____

_____

Inspire

> Dwell on the beauty of life. Watch the stars, and see yourself running with them.
> **—Marcus Aurelius**

⬤ Action for Mindset Change

Date:

Gratitude Log

1. _____
_____

2. _____
_____

3. _____
_____

4. _____
_____

5. _____
_____

Day Thirty-Four

Show your gratefulness to someone today.

Day: ___ /40

Mindset Reading | Log

Read at least 30 minutes.
Write your one takeaway from that reading.

_____
_____
_____
_____
_____
_____

Inspire

I'm grateful for always this moment, the now, no matter what form it takes.
—Eckhart Tolle

Action for Mindset Change

Date:

Gratitude Log

1. _____

_____

2. _____

_____

3. _____

_____

4. _____

_____

5. _____

_____

Day Thirty-Five

Find three people to compliment today.

Day: /40

Mindset Reading — Log

Read at least 30 minutes.
Write your one takeaway from that reading.

_____
_____
_____
_____
_____
_____

Inspire

> Humor is mankind's greatest blessing.
> —Mark Twain

Action for Mindset Change

Date:

Gratitude Log

1. _____
   _____

2. _____
   _____

3. _____
   _____

4. _____
   _____

5. _____
   _____

Day Thirty-Six

This is just the beginning;
find a way to keep it going.

Day: /40

Mindset Reading — Log

Read at least 30 minutes.
Write your one takeaway from that reading.

_____

_____

_____

_____

_____

_____

Inspire

Do not spoil what you have by desiring what you have not; remember that what you now have was once among the things you only hoped for.

–Epicurus

Action for Mindset Change

Date:

Gratitude Log

1. _____
   _____

2. _____
   _____

3. _____
   _____

4. _____
   _____

5. _____
   _____

Day Thirty-Seven

Are you looking forward to this each day?

Day: /40

Mindset Reading — Log

Read at least 30 minutes.
Write your one takeaway from that reading.

___

Inspire

> Let us be grateful to people who make us happy, they are the charming gardeners who make our souls blossom.
> **—Marcel Proust**

Action for Mindset Change

Date:

Gratitude Log

1. _____

_____

2. _____

_____

3. _____

_____

4. _____

_____

5. _____

_____

Day Thirty-Eight

Your mental mindset is changing,
even if you don't realize it.

Day: ___ /40

Mindset Reading | Log

Read at least 30 minutes.
Write your one takeaway from that reading.

_____

_____

_____

_____

_____

_____

Inspire

> Folks are usually about as happy as
> they make their minds up to be.
> **—Abraham Lincoln**

Action for Mindset Change

Date:

Gratitude Log

1. _____
_____

2. _____
_____

3. _____
_____

4. _____
_____

5. _____
_____

Day Thirty-Nine

You are an amazing person!

Day: /40

Mindset Reading — Log

Read at least 30 minutes.
Write your one takeaway from that reading.

_____
_____
_____
_____
_____
_____
_____

Inspire

Now and then it's good to pause in our pursuit of happiness and just be happy.
—Guillaume Apollinaire

Action for Mindset Change

Date: _____

Gratitude Log

1. _____
   _____

2. _____
   _____

3. _____
   _____

4. _____
   _____

5. _____
   _____

Day Forty

You have completely changed who you are forever. You will see!

Blessings,
Alice

| Day: | /40 |

Mindset Reading — Log

Read at least 30 minutes.
Write your one takeaway from that reading.

_____
_____
_____
_____
_____
_____
_____

Inspire

As we express our gratitude, we must never forget that the highest appreciation is not to utter words but to live by them.
—John F. Kennedy

Action for Mindset Change

You did it!

You made a committment and stuck to it.

You've lived 40 days finding and focusing on your gratitude EVERY DAY.
You've changed your mindset to one of gratitude—now change your life!

Resources

Use these resources for further mindset and accountability reading.

John C. Maxwell
Today Matters
Winning with People
Talent Is Never Enough
The 15 Invaluable Laws of Growth

Stephen R. Covey
The 7 Habits of Highly Effective People
The 8th Habit
First Things First

Bob Buford
Half Time

Kevin W. McCarthy
The On-Purpose Person

Robert S. McGee
The Search for Significance

Rick Warren
The Purpose Driven Life

Napolean Hill
Think and Grow Rich

James Allen
As a Man Thinketh

Dale Carnegie
How to Win Friends & Influence People

Bob Shank
Total Life Management

Shad Helmstetter, PhD
What to Say When You Talk to Yourself

Chrissy Metz
This Is Me: Loving the Person You Are Today

Vernice Armour
Zero to Breakthrough

Dan S. Kennedy
No B.S. Time Management for Entrepreneurs

Dani Johnson
First Steps to Wealth
Spirit Driven Success

Jim Rohn
All his books are good. Search for him on Google.

Tony Robbins
Unleash the Power Within

T. Harv Eker
Secrets of the Millionaire Mind

Prefer watching or listening?
Use YouTube or iTunes to find readings, speeches, or podcasts by these authors.

www.ingramcontent.com/pod-product-compliance
Lightning Source LLC
LaVergne TN
LVHW051604080426
835510LV00020B/3128